# Poems

*to help you through the week*

Text compiled by Andrea Skevington
This edition copyright © 2004 Lion Publishing

Published by
**Lion Publishing plc**
Mayfield House, 256 Banbury Road,
Oxford OX2 7DH, England
www.lion-publishing.co.uk
ISBN 0 7459 4853 7

First edition 2004
1 3 5 7 9 10 8 6 4 2 0

A catalogue record for this book is available
from the British Library

Typeset in 12/15 Lapidary 333
Printed and bound in Finland

# Poems

## to help you through the week

Compiled by
Andrea Skevington

A LION BOOK

Church-bells beyond the stars heard,

the soul's blood,

The land of spices: something understood.

*George Herbert*

# Contents

Introduction   6

Monday   9

Tuesday   25

Wednesday   43

Thursday   59

Friday   77

Saturday   95

Sunday   109

First line index   124

Author index   127

Acknowledgments   128

# Introduction

*Poems to Help You Through the Week* aims to do just that. The poems are full of everyday wonders: waking up, seeing a friend, finishing your work, or watching a young child walk. They help us to see beyond the busyness to those moments when heaven breaks through and touches us. There are poems, too, for when hope and help seem impossibly far away. The simple knowledge that others have felt something like our pain can help us to feel less alone, and more able to hear words of comfort. The poets may come from different places and different times, but the poems themselves show our common humanity.

The book has been set out so that it can be used in different ways. There is a section for every day of the week, and the reader can work through day by day. Also, each day has its own theme, within which the poems seem to speak to each other and follow trains of thought. This makes it easier to find poems that will help, whatever the circumstances.

Monday's theme is Morning. Waking up, walking to work, and watching the dawn are celebrated in poems to help you start the week.

Tuesday's poems are on Hope: looking forward to spring and happier times. They will help, too, when hope is hardest, and most necessary.

Wednesday's theme is Time: evoking the power of memory, as well as our anxieties about time slipping away. There are also poems to help us steady our perspective and remember our eternal Father.

Thursday's poems are full of Joy. They will lift the most jaded Thursday mood and inspire us to be thankful.

Friday's theme is Love: remembering what really matters. It ranges from the longing of young love to a contented marriage; and from the love for a child to the love of God.

Saturday's theme is Evening: from returning home and sitting by the fire, to those dark hours when help seems far away.

Sunday's poems are on Peace: they breathe contentment and tranquillity, restoring and reviving us. They remind us, too, where peace can be found.

# Morning

Angels, in the early morning

May be seen the Dews among,

Stooping – plucking – smiling – flying –

Do the Buds to them belong?

*Emily Dickinson*

## Coming Awake

When I woke, the lake-lights were quivering on the wall,
The sunshine swam in a shoal across and across,
And a hairy, big bee hung over the primulas
In the window, his body black fur,
   and the sound of him cross.

There was something I ought to remember: and yet
I did not remember. Why should I? The running lights
And the airy primulas, oblivious
Of the impending bee – they were fair enough sights.

*D.H. Lawrence*

## *Upon Westminster Bridge*

Earth has not anything to show more fair:
Dull would he be of soul who could pass by
A sight so touching in its majesty:
This City now doth, like a garment, wear
The beauty of the morning; silent, bare,
Ships, towers, domes, theatres, and temples lie
Open unto the fields, and to the sky;
All bright and glittering in the smokeless air.
Never did sun more beautifully steep
In his first splendour, valley, rock, or hill;
Ne'er saw I, never felt, a calm so deep!
The river glideth at his own sweet will:
Dear God! The very houses seem asleep;
And all that mighty heart is lying still!

*William Wordsworth*

## From *The Excursion*

What soul was his, when, from the naked top
Of some bold headland, he beheld the sun
Rise up, and bathe the world in light!
    He looked –
Ocean and earth, the solid frame of earth
And ocean's liquid mass, in gladness lay
Beneath him: Far and wide the clouds were touched,
And in their silent faces could he read
Unutterable love. Sound needed none,
Nor any voice of joy; his spirit drank
The spectacle: sensation, soul and form,
All melted into him; they swallowed up
His animal being; in them did he live;
And by them did he live: they were his life.
In such access of mind, in such high hour
Of visitation from the living God
Thought was not; in enjoyment it expired.
No thanks he breathed, he proffered no request;
Rapt into still communion that transcends
The imperfect offices of prayer and praise.

His mind was a thanksgiving to the power
That made him; it was blessedness and love!

*William Wordsworth*

## Psalm 19:1–5

The heavens declare the glory of God;
the skies proclaim the work of his hands.
Day after day they pour forth speech;
night after night they display knowledge.
There is no speech or language
where their voice is not heard.
Their voice goes out into all the earth,
their words to the ends of the world.

In the heavens he has pitched a tent for the sun,
which is like a bridegroom coming forth from his pavilion,
like a champion rejoicing to run his course.

*The Bible*

**Monday**

## This and My Heart

It's all I have to bring today –
This, and my heart beside –
This, and my heart, and all the fields –
And all the meadows wide –
Be sure you count – should I forget
Someone the sum could tell –
This, and my heart, and all the Bees
Which in the Clover dwell.

*Emily Dickinson*

## *God of the Morning*

God of the morning, at whose voice
The cheerful sun makes haste to rise,
And like a giant doth rejoice
To run his journey through the skies;

O, like the sun, may I fulfil
The appointed duties of the day,
With ready mind and active will
March on, and keep my heavenly way.

Give me thy counsel for my guide,
And then receive me to thy bliss:
All my desires and hopes beside
Are faint and cold, compared with this.

*Isaac Watts*

## London Snow

When men were all asleep the snow came flying,
In large white flakes falling on the city brown,
Stealthily and perpetually settling and loosely lying,
Hushing the latest traffic of the drowsy town;
Deadening, muffling, stifling its murmurs failing;
Lazily and incessantly floating down and down:
Silently sifting and veiling road, roof and railing;
Hiding difference, making unevenness even,
Into angles and crevices softly drifting and sailing.
All night it fell, and when full inches seven
It lay in depth of its uncompacted lightness,
The clouds blew off from a high and frosty heaven;
And all woke earlier for the unaccustomed brightness
Of the winter dawning, the strange unheavenly glare:
The eye marvelled – marvelled at the dazzling whiteness;
The ear hearkened to the stillness of the solemn air;
No sound of wheel rumbling nor of foot falling,
And the busy morning cries came thin and spare.
The boys I heard, as they went to school, calling,
They gathered up the crystal manna to freeze

Their tongues with tasting, their hands with snowballing;
Or rioted in a drift, plunging up to the knees;
Or peering up from under the white-mossed wonder
'O look at the trees!' they cried, 'O look at the trees!'
With lessened load a few carts creak and blunder,
Following along the white deserted way,
A country company long dispersed asunder:
When now already the sun, in pale display
Standing by Paul's high dome, spread forth below
His sparkling beams, and awoke the stir of the day.
For now doors open, and war is waged with the snow;
And trains of sombre men, past tale of number,
Tread long brown paths, as toward their toil they go:
But even for them awhile no cares encumber
Their minds diverted; the daily word is unspoken,
The daily thoughts of labour and sorrow slumber
At the sight of the beauty that greets them,
    for the charm they have broken.

*Robert Bridges*

Monday

17

## Happiness

So early it's still almost dark out.
I'm near the window with coffee,
and the usual early morning stuff
that passes for thought.
When I see the boy and his friend
walking up the road
to deliver the newspaper.
They wear caps and sweaters,
and one boy has a bag over his shoulder.
They are so happy
they aren't saying anything, these boys.
I think if they could, they would take
each other's arm.
It's early in the morning,
and they are doing this thing together.
They come on, slowly.
The sky is taking on light,
though the moon still hangs pale over the water.

Such beauty that for a minute
death and ambition, even love,
doesn't enter into this.
Happiness. It comes on
unexpectedly. And goes beyond, really,
any early morning talk about it.

*Raymond Carver*

## *Hallelujah Chorus*

Oh, you gotta get a glory
In the work you do;
A Hallelujah chorus
In the heart of you.

Paint, or tell a story,
Sing, or shovel coal,
But you gotta get a glory,
Or the job lacks soul.

*Anonymous American song*

**Monday**

## From *The Things That Matter*

Now that I've nearly done my days,
And grown too stiff to sweep or sew,
I sit and think, till I'm amaze,
About what lots of things I know:
Things as I've found out one by one –
And when I'm fast down in the clay,
My knowing things and how they're done
Will all be lost and thrown away.

There's things, I know, as won't be lost,
Things as folks write and talk about:
The way to keep your roots from frost,
And how to get your ink spots out.
What medicine's good for sores and sprains,
What way to salt your butter down,
What charms will cure your different pains,
And what will bright your faded gown.

But more important things than these,
They can't be written in a book:
How fast to boil your greens and peas,
And how good bacon ought to look;
The feel of real good wearing stuff,
The kind of apple as will keep,
The look of bread that's rose enough,
And how to get a child asleep.

Forgetting seems such silly waste!
I know so many little things,
And now the Angels will make haste
To dust it all away with wings!
O God, you made me like to know,
You kept the things straight in my head,
Please God, if you can make it so,
Let me know *something* when I'm dead!

*Edith Nesbit*

## Autumn

The morns are meeker than they were –
The nuts are getting brown –
The berry's cheek is plumper –
The Rose is out of town.

The Maple wears a gayer scarf –
The field a scarlet gown –
Lest I should be old-fashioned
I'll put a trinket on.

*Emily Dickinson*

## From *Lines Written at a Small Distance from My House*

It is the first mild day of March:
Each minute sweeter than before,
The redbreast sings from the tall larch
That stands beside our door.

There is a blessing in the air,
Which seems a sense of joy to yield
To the bare trees, and mountains bare,
And grass in the green field.

My sister! ('tis a wish of mine)
Now that our morning meal is done,
Make haste, your morning task resign;
Come forth and feel the sun.

*William Wordsworth*

**Monday**

# Hope

## *Thaw*

Over the land freckled with snow half-thawed

The speculating rooks at their nest cawed

And saw from elm-tops, delicate as flower of grass,

What we below could not see, Winter pass.

*Edward Thomas*

## The First Spring Day

I wonder if the sap is stirring yet,
If wintry birds are dreaming of a mate,
If frozen snowdrops feel as yet the sun
And crocus fires are kindling one by one:
  Sing, robin, sing;
I still am sore in doubt concerning Spring.

I wonder if the springtide of this year
Will bring another Spring both lost and dear;
If heart and spirit will find out their Spring,
Or if the world alone will bud and sing:
  Sing, hope, to me;
Sweet notes, my hope, soft notes for memory.

The sap will surely quicken soon or late,
The tardiest bird will twitter to a mate;
So Spring must dawn again with warmth and bloom,
Or in this world, or in the world to come:
  Sing, voice of Spring,
Till I too blossom and rejoice and sing.

*Christina Rossetti*

## *Joel 2:21–24*

Be not afraid, O land;

be glad and rejoice.

Surely the Lord has done great things.

Be not afraid, O wild animals,

for the open pastures are becoming green.

The trees are bearing their fruit;

the fig-tree and the vine yield their riches.

Be glad, O people of Zion,

rejoice in the Lord your God,

for he has given you the autumn rains in righteousness.

He sends you abundant showers,

both autumn and spring rains, as before.

The threshing-floors will be filled with grain;

the vats will overflow with new wine and oil.

*The Bible*

## Out Under the Sky

I wonder as I wander, out under the sky,
How Jesus the saviour did come for to die
For poor or'n'ry people like you and like I.
I wonder as I wander out under the sky.

When Mary bore Jesus, 'twas in a cow's stall,
With wise men and an'mals and shepherds and all.
But high from the heavens a star's light did fall,
And the promise of ages it then did recall.

If Jesus had wanted for any small thing,
A star in the sky or a bird on the wing,
Or all of God's angels in heav'n for to sing,
He could sure have had it, 'cause he was the King.

I wonder as I wander, out under the sky,
How Jesus the saviour did come for to die
For poor or'n'ry people like you and like I.
I wonder as I wander out under the sky.

*Traditional North Carolina carol*

## Hope

'Hope' is a thing with feathers –
That perches in the soul –
And sings the tune without the words –
And never stops – at all –

And sweetest – in the Gale – is heard –
And sore must be the storm –
That could abash the little Bird
That kept so many warm –

I've heard it in the chillest land –
And on the strangest Sea –
Yet, never, in Extremity,
It asked a crumb – of Me.

*Emily Dickinson*

## *Consider*

Consider

The lilies of the field whose bloom is brief:

   We are as they;

   Like them we fade away,

As doth a leaf.

Consider

The sparrows of the air of small account:

   Our God doth view

   Whether they fall or mount –

He guards us too.

Consider

The lilies that do neither spin nor toil,

   Yet are most fair:

   What profits all this care

And all this coil?

Consider

The birds that have no barn nor harvest-weeks;

    God gives them food:

    Much more our Father seeks

To do us good.

*Christina Rossetti*

## *When Time Is Over*

I shall know why – when Time is over –
And I have ceased to wonder why –
Christ will explain each separate anguish
In the fair schoolroom of the sky –

He will tell me what 'Peter' promised –
And I – for wonder at his woe –
I shall forget the drop of Anguish
That scalds me now – that scalds me now!

*Emily Dickinson*

## On the Grasshopper and Cricket

The poetry of earth is never dead:
When all the birds are faint with the hot sun
And hide in cooling trees, a voice will run
From hedge to hedge about the new-mown mead:
That is the grasshopper's – he takes the lead
In summer luxury – he had never done
With his delights, for when tired out with fun,
He rests at ease beneath some pleasant weed.
The poetry of earth is ceasing never:
On a lone winter evening, when the frost
Has wrought a silence, from the stove there shrills
The Cricket's song, in warmth increasing ever,
And seems to one in drowsiness half lost,
The Grasshopper's among some grassy hills.

*John Keats*

## The Other

There are nights that are so still
that I can hear the small owl calling
far off and a fox barking
miles away. It is then that I lie
in the lean hours awake listening
to the swell born somewhere in the Atlantic
rising and falling, rising and falling
wave on wave on the long shore
by the village, that is without light
and companionless. And the thought comes
of that other being who is awake, too,
letting our prayers break on him,
not like this for a few hours,
but for days, years, for eternity.

*R.S. Thomas*

## On His Blindness

When I consider how my light is spent,
Ere half my days, in this dark world and wide,
And that one talent which is death to hide
Lodged in me useless, though my soul more bent
To serve therewith my Maker, and present
My true account, lest he returning chide,
'Doth God exact day-labour, light denied?'
I fondly ask. But Patience, to prevent
That murmur, soon replies: 'God doth not need
Either man's work or his own gifts: who best
Bear his mild yoke, they serve him best. His state
Is kingly: thousands at his bidding speed,
And post o'er land and ocean without rest;
They also serve who only stand and wait.'

*John Milton*

## The Little Boy Lost

Father, father, where are you going
O do not walk so fast.
Speak father, speak to your little boy
Or else I shall be lost.

The night was dark no father was there
The child was wet with dew.
The mire was deep, and the child did weep
And away the vapour flew.

## The Little Boy Found

The little boy lost in the lonely fen,
Led by the wand'ring light,
Began to cry, but God ever nigh,
Appeared like his father in white.

He kissed the child and by the hand led
And to his mother brought,
Who in sorrow pale, thro' the lonely dale
Her little boy weeping sought.

*William Blake*

Tuesday

## In Hospital

Would I might lie like this, without the pain,
    For seven years – as one with snowy hair,
Who in the high tower dreams his dying reign –

    Lie here and watch the walls – how grey and bare,
The metal bed-post, the uncoloured screen,
    The mat, the jug, the cupboard, and the chair;

And served by an old woman, calm and clean,
    Her misted face familiar, yet unknown,
Who comes in silence, and departs unseen.

    And with no other visit, lie alone,
Nor stir, except I had my food to find
    In that dull bowl Diogenes might own.

And down my window I would draw the blind,
    And never look without, but, waiting, hear
A noise of rain, a whistling of the wind,

And only know that flame-foot Spring is near
By trilling birds, or by the patch of sun
    Crouching behind my curtains. So, in fear,

Noon-dreams should enter, softly, one by one,
    And throng about the floor, and float and play
And flicker on the screen, while minutes run –

    The last majestic minutes of the day –
And with the mystic shadows, Shadow grow.
    Then the grey square of wall should fade away,

And glow again, and open, and disclose
    The shimmering lake in which the planets swim,
And all that lake a dewdrop on a rose.

*James Elroy Flecker*

## Light Shining Out of Darkness

God moves in a mysterious way,
His wonders to perform;
He plants his footsteps in the sea,
And rides upon the storm.

Deep in unfathomable mines
Of never-failing skill
He treasures up his bright designs,
And works his sovereign will.

Ye fearful saints, fresh courage take,
The clouds ye so much dread
Are big with mercy, and shall break
In blessings on your head.

Judge not the Lord by feeble sense,
But trust him for his grace;
Behind a frowning providence,
He hides a smiling face.

His purposes will ripen fast,
Unfolding every hour;
The bud may have a bitter taste,
But sweet will be the flower.

Blind unbelief is sure to err,
And scan his work in vain;
God is his own interpreter,
And he will make it plain.

*William Cowper*

## The Door

Go and open the door.
  Maybe outside there's
  a tree, or a wood,
  a garden,
  or a magic city.

Go and open the door.
  Maybe a dog's rummaging.
  Maybe you'll see a face,
or an eye,
or the picture
            of a picture.

Go and open the door.
  If there's a fog
  it will clear.

Go and open the door.
        Even if there's only
        the darkness ticking,
        even if there's only
        the hollow wind,
        even if

nothing

            is there,

go and open the door.

At least

there'll be

a draft.

*Miroslav Holub, translated by Ian Milner*


## *Joel 2:25–26*

I'll make up for the years of the locust,

the great locust devastation –

Locusts savage, locusts deadly,

fierce locusts, locusts of doom,

that great locust invasion I sent your way.

You'll eat your fill of good food.

You'll be full of praises to your God,

the God who has set you back on your heels in wonder.

Never again will my people be despised.

*The Bible*

# Time

For whatsoever from one place doth fall

Is with the tide unto another brought:

For there is nothing lost, that may be found, if sought.

*Edmund Spenser*

## Sunday Teatime – Pen-y-groes

I remember that room so clearly.

My last visit,

Although I didn't know, then.

The room was dark,

Peaceful among voices.

Rich browns of paint and polish.

The black kettle over the fire.

The tick of a clock.

Two voices speaking in

Two tongues of

Times far back,

Tunnel-dark under the earth.

The smell of coal.

The smell of baking.

The table spread.

A gold-brown velvet cloth

Topped with creamy-white lace.

Best china – edged with

Gold like an open Bible. Quiet.

While through the window were

Row after row of cabbages and leeks
And tomatoes, waiting in the green sun.
The hen house was empty.
'They used to scratch and cluck,'
They said, and smiled.
So much, so much is left behind.

*Andrea Skevington*


## From *The World*

I saw Eternity the other night
Like a great Ring of pure and endless light,
    All calm as it was bright;
And round beneath it, Time, in hours, days, years,
    Driven by the spheres,
Like a vast shadow moved, in which the world
    And all her train were hurled.

*Henry Vaughan*

## Piano

Softly, in the dusk, a woman is singing to me;
Taking me back down the vista of years, till I see
A child sitting under the piano,
    in the boom of the tingling strings
And pressing the small, poised feet of a mother
    who smiles as she sings.

In spite of myself, the insidious mastery of song
Betrays me back, till the heart of me weeps to belong
To the old Sunday evenings at home, with winter outside
And hymns in the cosy parlour,
    the tinkling piano our guide.

So now it is vain for the singer to burst into clamour
With the great black piano appassionato. The glamour
Of childish days is upon me, my manhood is cast
Down in the flood of remembrance,
    I weep like a child for the past.

*D.H. Lawrence*

## Persuasion

'Man's life is like a Sparrow, mighty King!
That – while at banquet with your Chiefs you sit
Housed near a blazing fire – is seen to flit
Safe from the wintry tempest. Fluttering,
Here did it enter; there, on hasty wing,
Flies out, and passes on from cold to cold;
But whence it came we know not, nor behold
Whither it goes. Even such, that transient Thing,
The human Soul; not utterly unknown
While in the Body lodged, her warm abode;
But from what world She came, what woe or weal
On her departure waits, no tongue hath shown;
This mystery if the Stranger can reveal,
His be a welcome cordially bestowed!'

*William Wordsworth*

## Where the Picnic Was

Where we made the fire
In the summer time
Of branch and briar
On the hill to the sea,
I slowly climb
Through winter mire,
And scan and trace
The forsaken place
Quite readily.

Now a cold wind blows,
And the grass is grey,
But the spot still shows
As a burnt circle – aye,
And stick-ends, charred,
Still strew the sward
Whereon I stand,
Last relic of the band
Who came that day!

Yes, I am here
Just as last year,
And the sea breathes brine
From its strange straight line
Up hither, the same
As when we four came.
– But two have wandered far
From this grassy rise
Into urban roar
Where no picnics are,
And one – has shut her eyes
For evermore.

*Thomas Hardy*

## Sonnet 30

When to the sessions of sweet silent thought
I summon up remembrance of things past,
I sigh the lack of many a thing I sought,
And with old woes new wail my dear time's waste:
Then can I drown an eye, unused to flow,
For precious friends hid in death's dateless night,
And weep afresh love's long since cancelled woe,
And moan th'expense of many a vanished sight:
Then can I grieve at grievances foregone,
And heavily from woe to woe tell o'er
The sad account of fore-bemoaned moan,
Which I new pay as if not paid before.
But if the while I think on thee, dear friend,
All losses are restored, and sorrows end.

*William Shakespeare*

**Wednesday**

## Psalm 103:13–17

As a father has compassion on his children,
so the Lord has compassion on those who fear him;
for he knows how we are formed,
he remembers that we are dust.
As for man, his days are like grass,
he flourishes like a flower of the field;
the wind blows over it and it is gone,
and its place remembers it no more.
But from everlasting to everlasting
the Lord's love is with those who fear him,
and his righteousness with their children's children.

*The Bible*

## *The Bright Field*

I have seen the sun break through
to illuminate a small field
for a while, and gone my way
and forgotten it. But that was the pearl
of great price, the one field that had
the treasure in it. I realize now
that I must give all that I have
to possess it. Life is not hurrying

on to a receding future, nor hankering after
an imagined past. It is the turning
aside like Moses to the miracle
of the lit bush, to a brightness
that seemed as transitory as your youth
once, but is the eternity that awaits you.

R.S. Thomas

## *Ecclesiastes 3:1–8*

For everything there is a season,
and a time for every matter under heaven:
a time to be born, and a time to die;
a time to plant, and a time to pluck up what is planted;
a time to kill, and a time to heal;
a time to break down, and a time to build up;
a time to weep, and a time to laugh;
a time to mourn, and a time to dance;
a time to cast away stones,
    and a time to gather stones together;
a time to embrace, and a time to refrain from embracing;
a time to seek, and a time to lose;
a time to keep, and a time to cast away;
a time to rend, and a time to sew;
a time to keep silence, and a time to speak;
a time to love, and a time to hate;
a time for war, and a time for peace.

*The Bible*

**Wednesday**

## How No Age Is Content with His Own Estate

Laid in my quiet bed, in study as I were,

I saw within my troubled head a heap of thoughts appear.

And every thought did show so lively in mine eyes,

That now I sighed, and then I smiled,

    as cause of thought doth rise.

I saw the little boy in thought how oft that he

Did wish of God to scape the rod, a tall young man to be.

The young man eke that feels his bones

    with pains oppressed,

How he would be a rich old man, to live and lie at rest.

The rich old man that sees his end draw on so sore,

How he would be a boy again, to live so much the more.

Whereat full oft I smiled, to see how all these three,

From boy to man, from man to boy

    would chop and change degree.

*Henry Howard*

## From *Last Lesson of the Afternoon*

When will the bell ring, and end this weariness?
How long have they tugged the leash, and strained apart,
My pack of unruly hounds! I cannot start
Them again on a quarry of knowledge they hate to hunt,
I can haul them and urge them no more.

I do not, and will not; they won't and they don't;
    and that's all!
I shall keep my strength for myself;
    they can keep theirs as well.
Why should we beat our heads against the wall
Of each other? I shall sit and wait for the bell.

*D.H. Lawrence*

## Old Age

The seas are quiet when the winds give o'er;
So calm are we when passions are no more.
For then we know how vain it was to boast
Of fleeting things, so certain to be lost.
Clouds of affection from our younger eyes
Conceal that emptiness which age descries.

The soul's dark cottage, battered and decayed,
Lets in new light through chinks that Time has made:
Stronger by weakness, wiser men become
As they draw near to their eternal home.
Leaving the old, both worlds at once they view
That stand upon the threshold of the new.

*Edmund Waller*

# From *Maud; A Monodrama*

Ah, what shall I be at fifty
Should Nature keep me alive,
If I find the world so bitter
When I am but twenty-five?

*Alfred, Lord Tennyson*


# *Epigram*

My soul, sit thou a patient looker-on;
Judge not the play before the play is done:
Her plot has many changes; every day
Speaks a new scene; the last act crowns the play.

*Francis Quarles*

# Joy

## *Eternity*

He who bends to himself a joy
Does its winged life destroy;
But he who kisses the joy as it flies
Lives in eternity's sunrise.

*William Blake*

## Piping Down the Valleys Wild

Piping down the valleys wild,
Piping songs of pleasant glee,
On a cloud I saw a child,
And he laughing said to me:

'Pipe a song about a Lamb!'
So I piped with merry cheer.
'Piper, pipe that song again.'
So I piped: he wept to hear.

'Drop thy pipe, thy happy pipe,
Sing thy songs of happy cheer.'
So I sung the same again,
While he wept with joy to hear.

'Piper, sit thee down and write
In a book, that all may read.'
So he vanished from my sight,
And I plucked a hollow reed,

And I made a rural pen,
And I stained the water clear,
And I wrote my happy songs
Every child may joy to hear.

*William Blake*

## *Summer Air*

A soft Sea washed around the House
A Sea of Summer Air
And rose and fell the magic Planks
That sailed without a care –
For Captain was the Butterfly
For Helmsman was the Bee
And an entire universe
For the delighted crew.

*Emily Dickinson*

## Pied Beauty

Glory be to God for dappled things –
For skies of couple-colour as a brinded cow;
For rose-moles all in stipple upon trout that swim;
Fresh-firecoal chestnut-falls; finches' wings;
Landscape plotted and pieced – fold, fallow, and plough;
And all trades, their gear and tackle and trim.

All things counter, original, spare, strange;
Whatever is fickle, freckled (who knows how?)
With swift, slow; sweet, sour; adazzle, dim;
He fathers-forth whose beauty is past change:
    Praise him.

*Gerard Manley Hopkins*

## This Is the Spot

This is the spot: how mildly does the sun
Shine in between the fading leaves! The air
In the habitual silence of this wood
Is more than silent; and this bed of heath –
Where shall we find so sweet a resting place?
Come, let me see thee sink into a dream
Of quiet thoughts, protracted till thine eye
Be calm as water when the winds are gone
And no one can tell whither. My sweet Friend,
We two have had such happy hours together
That my heart melts in me to think of it.

*William Wordsworth*

## Blessings

The storm has passed.
The sky shines clear blue,
Alive with the swoop and cry of swallows.
Lazy in the garden stands the plum tree
Its branches bent with fruit,
Rich red and touched by the sun.
Tomorrow they will be ready,
When the cool mist ebbs, and
The sun has dried them.
We will climb the ladder and
Laughing pick them all – all we can reach –
And boil them dangerously as
The sweet steam rises.
In jars they will sit,
Shining like the summer sun,
Glowing clear and ruby red.

**Thursday**

One by one the jars will be eaten,

As the days shorten, and

Darkness draws near.

We will remember the laughter,

And the swoop of swallows.

*Andrea Skevington*


## From *The Garden*

What wondrous life is this I lead!

Ripe apples drop about my head;

The luscious clusters of the vine

Upon my mouth do crush their wine;

The nectarine and curious peach

Into my hands themselves do reach;

Stumbling on melons, as I pass,

Ensnared with flowers, I fall on grass.

*Andrew Marvell*

**Thursday**

## For the Beauty of the Earth

For the beauty of the earth,
For the beauty of the skies,
For the love which from our birth
Over and around us lies,
Lord of all, to thee we raise
This our grateful hymn of praise.

For the beauty of each hour
Of the day and of the night,
Hill and vale, and tree and flower,
Sun and moon and stars of light,
Lord of all, to thee we raise,
This our grateful hymn of praise.

For the joy of human love,
Brother, sister, parent, child,
Friends on earth, and friends above,
Pleasures pure and undefiled,
Lord of all, to thee we raise
This our grateful hymn of praise.

**Thursday**

For each perfect gift of thine,

To our race so freely given,

Graces human and divine,

Flowers of earth and buds of heaven,

Lord of all, to thee we raise,

This our grateful hymn of praise.

*F.S. Pierpoint*

## The Character of a Happy Life

How happy is he born and taught
That serveth not another's will;
Whose armour is his honest thought,
And simple truth his utmost skill!

Whose passions not his masters are;
Whose soul is still prepared for death,
Untied unto the world by care
Of public fame or private breath;

Who envies none that chance doth raise,
Nor vice; who never understood
How deepest wounds are given by praise;
Nor rules of state, but rules of good;

Who hath his life from rumours freed;
Whose conscience is his strong retreat;
Whose state can neither flatterers feed,
Nor ruin make oppressors great;

Who God doth late and early pray
More of His grace than gifts to lend;
And entertains the harmless day
With a religious book or friend;

This man is freed from servile bands
Of hope to rise or fear to fall:
Lord of himself, though not of lands,
And having nothing, yet hath all.

*Sir Henry Wotton*

Thursday

## Psalm 92:1–5

It is good to praise the Lord
and make music to your name, O Most High,
to proclaim your love in the morning
and your faithfulness at night,
to the music of the ten-stringed lyre
and the melody of the harp.

For you make me glad by your deeds, O Lord;
I sing for joy at the work of your hands.
How great are your works, O Lord,
how profound your thoughts!

*The Bible*

## Prayer

Prayer the Church's banquet, angels' age,
God's breath in man returning to his birth,
The soul in paraphrase, heart in pilgrimage,
The Christian plummet sounding heaven and earth;
Engine against th'Almighty, sinner's tower,
Reversed thunder, Christ-side-piercing spear,
The six-days world transposing in an hour,
A kind of tune, which all things hear and fear;
Softness, and peace, and joy, and love, and bliss,
Exalted manna, gladness of the best,
Heaven in ordinary, man well dressed,
The milky way, the bird of Paradise,
Church-bells beyond the stars heard, the soul's blood,
The land of spices: something understood.

*George Herbert*

## Laughing Song

When the green woods laugh with the voice of joy,
And the dimpling stream runs laughing by;
When the air does laugh with our merry wit,
And the green hill laughs with the noise of it;

When the meadows laugh with lively green,
And the grasshopper laughs in the merry scene;
When Mary and Susan and Emily
With their sweet round mouths sing 'Ha, ha, he!'

When the painted birds laugh in the shade,
When our table with cherries and nuts is spread:
Come live, and be merry, and join with me
To sing the sweet chorus of 'Ha, ha, he!'

*William Blake*

**Thursday**

## A Birthday

My heart is like a singing bird
Whose nest is in a watered shoot:
My heart is like an apple tree
Whose boughs are bent with thickset fruit;
My heart is like a rainbow shell
That paddles in a halcyon sea;
My heart is gladder than all these
Because my love is come to me.

Raise me a dais of silk and down;
Hang it with vair and purple dyes;
Carve it in doves and pomegranates,
And peacocks with a hundred eyes;
Work it in gold and silver grapes,
In leaves and silver fleurs-de-lys;
Because the birthday of my life
Is come, my love is come to me.

*Christina Rossetti*

## Digging

Today, I think
Only with scents – scents dead leaves yield,
And bracken, and wild carrot's seed,
And the square mustard field;

Odours that rise
When the spade wounds the root of tree,
Rose, currant, raspberry, or goutweed,
Rhubarb or celery;

The smoke's smell, too,
Flowing from where a bonfire burns
The dead, the waste, the dangerous,
And all to sweetness turns.

It is enough
To smell, to crumble the dark earth,
While the robin sings over again
Sad songs of autumn mirth.

*Edward Thomas*

## *Psalm 148:7–13*

Praise the Lord from the earth,

you great sea creatures and all ocean depths,

lightning and hail, snow and clouds,

stormy winds that do his bidding,

you mountains and all hills,

fruit trees and all cedars,

wild animals and all cattle,

small creatures and flying birds,

kings of the earth and all nations,

you princes and all rulers on earth,

young men and maidens,

old men and children.

Let them praise the name of the Lord,

for his name alone is exalted;

his splendour is above the earth and the heavens.

*The Bible*

# Love

## *Late Fragment*

And did you get what
you wanted from this life, even so?
I did.
And what did you want?
To call myself beloved, to feel myself
beloved on the earth.

*Raymond Carver*

## Meeting at Night

The grey sea and the long black land;
And the yellow half-moon large and low;
And the startled little waves that leap
In fiery ringlets from their sleep,
As I gain the cove with pushing prow,
And quench its speed i' the slushy sand.

Then a mile of warm sea-scented beach;
Three fields to cross till a farm appears;
A tap at the pane, the quick sharp scratch
And blue spurt of a lighted match,
And a voice less loud, through all its joys and fears,
Than the two hearts beating each to each!

*Robert Browning*

## Song of Songs 3:1; 5:2

All night long on my bed
I looked for the one my heart loves;
I looked for him but did not find him.

I slept but my heart was awake.
Listen! My lover is knocking:
'Open to me, my sister, my darling,
my dove, my flawless one.
My head is drenched with dew,
my hair with the dampness of the night.'

*The Bible*

## Up-hill

Does the road wind up-hill all the way?
    Yes, to the very end.
Will the day's journey take the whole long day?
    From morn to night, my friend.

But is there for the night a resting place?
    A roof for when the slow dark hours begin.
May not the darkness hide it from my face?
    You cannot miss that inn.

Shall I meet other wayfarers at night?
    Those who have gone before.
Then must I knock, or call when just in sight?
    They will not keep you standing at that door.

Shall I find comfort, travel-sore and weak?
    Of labour you shall find the sum.
Will there be beds for me and all who seek?
    Yea, beds for all who come.

*Christina Rossetti*

## Love

Love bade me welcome; yet my soul drew back,
    Guilty of dust and sin.
But quick-eyed Love, observing me grow slack
    From my first entrance in,
Drew nearer to me, sweetly questioning,
    If I lacked anything.

'A guest,' I answered, 'worthy to be here.'
    Love said, 'You shall be he.'
'I, the unkind, ungrateful? Ah, my dear,
    I cannot look on thee.'
Love took my hand, and smiling did reply,
    'Who made the eyes but I?'

'Truth, Lord, but I have marred them; let my shame
    Go where it doth deserve.'
'And know you not,' says Love, 'who bore the blame?'
    'My dear, then I will serve.'
'You must sit down,' says Love, 'and taste my meat.'
    So I did sit and eat.

*George Herbert*

Friday

## Easter

Most glorious Lord of life! That, on this day,
Didst make thy triumph over death and sin;
And, having harrowed hell, didst bring away
Captivity thence captive, us to win:
This joyous day, dear Lord, with joy begin;
And grant that we, for whom thou diddest die,
Being with thy dear blood clean washed from sin,
May live for ever in felicity!
And that thy love we weighing worthily,
May likewise love thee for the same again;
And for thy sake, that all like dear didst buy,
With love may one another entertain:
So let us love, dear Love, like as we ought;
Love is the lesson which the Lord us taught.

*Edmund Spenser*

**Friday**

# From *The Rime of the Ancient Mariner*

O sweeter than the marriage feast,
'Tis sweeter far to me
To walk together to the Kirk
With goodly company;

To walk together to the Kirk
And all together pray,
While each to his great Father bends,
Old men, and babes, and loving friends,
And youths, and maidens gay.

Farewell, farewell! But this I tell
To thee, thou wedding-guest!
He prayeth well who loveth well
Both man and bird and beast.

He prayeth best who loveth best
All things both great and small:
For the dear God, who loveth us,
He made and loveth all.

*Samuel Taylor Coleridge*

**Friday**

83

## Now You Will Feel No Rain

Now you will feel no rain,
for each of you will be a shelter to the other.

Now you will feel no cold,
for each of you will be warmth to the other.

Now there is no loneliness for you;
now there is no more loneliness.

Now you are two bodies,
but there is only one life before you.

Go now to your dwelling place,
to enter into your days together.

And may your days be good
and long on the earth.

*Apache song, translator unknown*

## *To My Dear and Loving Husband*

If ever two were one, then surely we.
If ever man were loved by wife, then thee;
If ever wife was happy in a man,
Compare with me, ye women, if you can.
I prize thy love more than whole mines of gold
Or all the riches that the East doth hold.
My love is such that rivers cannot quench,
Nor aught but love from thee give recompense.
Thy love is such I can no way repay,
The heavens reward thee manifold, I pray.
Then while we live, in love let's so persevere
That when we live no more, we may live ever.

*Anne Bradstreet*

## His Late Wife's Wedding Ring

The ring so worn, as you behold,
So thin, so pale, is yet of gold:
The passion such it was to prove:
Worn with life's cares, love yet was love.

*George Crabbe*


## Just in Sight

They might not need me, but they might.
I'll let my head be just in sight;
A smile as small as mine might be
Precisely their necessity.

*Emily Dickinson*

## To Joanna

Amid the smoke of cities did you pass

Your time of early youth; and there you learned,

From years of quiet industry, to love

The living beings by your own fireside

With such strong devotion, that your heart

Is slow towards the sympathies of them

Who look upon the hills with tenderness,

And make dear friendships with the streams and groves.

Yet we, who are transgressors in this kind,

Dwelling retired in our simplicity

Among the woods and field, we love you well,

Joanna! And I guess, since you have been

So distant from us now for two long years,

That you will gladly listen to discourse

However trivial, if you thence are taught

That they with whom you once were happy talk

Familiarly of you and of old times.

*William Wordsworth*

## *Baby Running Barefoot*

When the white feet of the baby beat across the grass
The little white feet nod like white flowers in a wind,
They poise and run like puffs of wind that pass
Over the water where the weeds are thinned.

And the sight of their white playing in the grass
Is winsome as a robin's song, so fluttering;
Or like two butterflies that settle on a glass
Cup for a moment, soft little wing-beats uttering.

And I wish that the baby would tack across here to me
Like a wind-shadow running on a pond, so she could stand
With two little bare white feet upon my knee
And I could feel her feet in either hand

Cool as syringa buds in morning hours
Or firm and silken as young peony flowers.

*D.H. Lawrence*

## Hosea 11:3–4

It was I who taught Ephraim to walk,

taking them by the arms;

but they did not realize

it was I who healed them.

I led them with cords of human kindness,

with ties of love;

I lifted the yoke from their neck

and bent down to feed them.

*The Bible*

## The View from Your Window

I remember before you were born,
Each of you,
Standing by this window,
Cradling you with one hand
And looking out.
Your eyes were closed then,
But not for long.
What would you see
Through this window?

I filled hangers with nuts and
Seeds, and planted a trough of
Flowers
For you to watch.
Now, you fill the hangers
Yourselves,
And know which
Birds come,
And which do not.

You planted the trough yesterday,
So full of bulbs there was

Scarcely room for soil.
You planted each other's
Favourite colours,
And laughed when you imagined
How it will look when the
Sun creeps round next spring.

I felt you tumble for joy
Before you were born,
Both of you,
And now look as you
Gasp at the soft pink dawn
Reflected in the river.
And watch the Sea of
Tranquillity shimmer
On a frosty night.
God has been painting again
You say.
He has, I reply.

*Andrea Skevington*

## Isaiah 43:1–2

But now, this is what the Lord says –

he who created you, O Jacob,

he who formed you, O Israel:

'Fear not, for I have redeemed you;

I have summoned you by name; you are mine.

When you pass through the waters,

I will be with you;

and when you pass through the rivers,

they will not sweep over you.

When you walk through the fire,

you will not be burned;

the flames will not set you ablaze.

*The Bible*

## From *The Divine Comedy*

The love of God, unutterable and perfect,
flows into a pure soul the way that light
rushes into a transparent object.
The more love that it finds, the more it gives
itself; so that, as we grow clear and open,
the more complete the joy of loving is.
And the more souls who resonate together,
the greater the intensity of their love,
for, mirror-like, each soul reflects the others.

*Dante Alighieri, translated by Stephen Mitchell*

**Friday**

.

# Evening

## From *Lines Written Above Tintern Abbey*

Therefore let the moon
Shine on thee in thy solitary walk;
And let the misty mountain winds be free
To blow against thee.

*William Wordsworth*

## Sowing

It was a perfect day
For sowing; just
As sweet and dry was the ground
As tobacco dust.

I tasted deep the hour
Between the far
Owl's chuckling first soft cry
And the first star.

A long stretched hour it was;
Nothing undone
Remained; the early seeds
All safely sown.

And now, hark at the rain,
Windless and light,
Half a kiss, half a tear,
Saying goodnight.

*Edward Thomas*

**Saturday**

# From *Elegy Written in a Country Churchyard*

The curfew tolls the knell of parting day,
The lowing herd wind slowly o'er the lea,
The ploughman homeward plods his weary way,
And leaves the world to darkness and to me.

Now fades the glimmering landscape on the sight,
And all the air a solemn stillness holds,
Save where the beetle wheels his droning flight,
And drowsy tinklings lull the distant folds;

Save that from yonder ivy-mantled tower
The moping owl does to the moon complain
Of such, as wandering near her secret bower,
Molest her ancient solitary reign.

Beneath those rugged elms, that yew tree's shade,
Where heaves the turf in many a mouldering heap,
Each in his narrow cell for ever laid,
The rude forefathers of the hamlet sleep.

*Thomas Gray*

## Snow at Dusk

Sky and grass – the same colour
at dusk. Frost-grey and heavy.
The trees, grey too, touch both.

The only clear thing is a path,
where first flakes of snow settle –
light on the stone-hard earth –
a white ribbon twisting
through trees.

The flakes fall more thickly now.
How can those clouds hold
so much white –
Falling
from the grey sky.
When it is gone,
the sky will be
as black as night.

The path, clear and white,
leads on, and we walk home,

boots trailing flakes

as soft as clouds

through snow-covered night.

*Andrea Skevington*


## *The Fallow Deer at the Lonely House*

One without looks in tonight

Through the curtain-chink

From the sheet of glistening white;

One without looks in tonight

As we sit and think

By the fender-brink.

We do not discern those eyes

Watching in the snow;

Lit by lamps of rosy dyes

We do not discern those eyes

Wondering, aglow,

Four-footed, tiptoe.

*Thomas Hardy*

## The Little Town at Evening

The chime of the bells, and the church clock striking eight
Solemnly and distinctly cries down the babel of children
    still playing in the hay.
The church draws nearer upon us, gentle and great
In the shadow, covering us up with her grey.

Like drowsy creatures, the houses fall asleep
Under the fleece of shadow, as in between
Tall and dark the church moves, anxious to keep
Their sleeping, cover them soft unseen.

Hardly a murmur comes from the sleeping brood;
I wish the church had covered me up with the rest
In the home-place. Why is it she should exclude
Me so distinctly from sleeping the sleep I'd love best?

*D.H. Lawrence*

**Saturday**

## Psalm 22:1–2

My God, my God, why have you forsaken me?

Why are you so far from saving me,

so far from the words of my groaning?

O my God, I cry out by day, but you do not answer,

by night, and am not silent.

*The Bible*


## From *The Visionary*

Silent is the house: all are laid asleep:

One alone looks out o'er the snow-wreaths deep,

Watching every cloud, dreading every breeze

That whirls the wildering drift,

    and bends the groaning trees.

Cheerful is the hearth, soft the matted floor;

Not one shivering gust creeps through pane or door;

The little lamp burns straight, its rays shoot strong and far:

I trim it well, to be the wanderer's guiding star.

*Emily Brontë*

## *Darkness*

We grow accustomed to the Dark –
When Light is put away –
As when the Neighbour holds the Lamp
To witness her Goodbye –

A Moment – We uncertain step
For newness of the night –
Then – fit our Vision to the Dark –
And meet the Road – erect –

And so of larger – Darknesses –
Those Evenings of the Brain –
When not a Moon disclose a sign –
Or Star – come out – within –

The Bravest – grope a little –
And sometimes hit a Tree
Directly in the Forehead –
But as they learn to see –

**Saturday**

Either the Darkness alters –
Or something in the sight
Adjusts itself to Midnight –
And Life steps almost straight.

*Emily Dickinson*

## *Psalm 139:11–12*

If I say, 'Surely the darkness will hide me
and the light become night around me,'
even the darkness will not be dark to you;
the night will shine like the day,
for darkness is as light to you.

*The Bible*

## Crossing the Bar

Sunset and evening star,
And one clear call for me!
And may there be no moaning of the bar,
When I put out to sea,

But such a tide as moving seems asleep,
Too full for sound and foam,
When that which drew from out the boundless deep
Turns again home.

Twilight and evening bell,
And after that the dark!
And may there be no sadness of farewell,
When I embark;

For though from out our bourne of Time and Place
The flood may bear me far,
I hope to see my pilot face to face
When I have crossed the bar.

*Alfred, Lord Tennyson*

**Saturday**

## Holy Sonnet 10

Death, be not proud, though some have called thee

Mighty and dreadful, for thou art not so;

For those whom thou think'st thou dost overthrow

Die not, poor Death, nor yet canst thou kill me.

From rest and sleep, which but thy pictures be,

Much pleasure – then from thee much more must flow;

And soonest our best men with thee do go,

Rest of their bones, and soul's delivery.

Thou art slave to fate, chance, kings, and desperate men,

And dost with poison, war, and sickness dwell;

And poppy or charms can make us sleep as well

And better than thy stroke; why swell'st thou then?

One short sleep past, we wake eternally,

And death shall be no more; Death, thou shalt die.

*John Donne*

## Light

Here, quiet on this stony shore, light
drains from the edges first. Blue deepens to blue,
leaving one pool of brightness against the night,

as the starlight, faint at first, shines bright
on the black waves that rise and fold,
here, quiet on this stony shore. Light

flecks the foam that trembles and shines white,
as the circle of darkness turns closer,
leaving one pool of brightness against the night.

Now, in the blackness, bright birds stop their flight
and shut their star-filled eyes against the dark.
Here, quiet on this stony shore, light

shines on white pebbles, shimmering and star-bright
as shadows seep and spread like tar rising,
leaving one pool of brightness against the night.

The stars, the foam, and the pebbles shine with light
that washes and wells and rises
here, quiet on this stony shore. Light
leaving one pool of brightness against the night.

*Andrea Skevington*


## From *Shadows*

And if tonight my soul may find her peace
in sleep, and sink in good oblivion,
and in the morning wake like a new-opened flower
then I have been dipped again in God, and new-created.
And if, as weeks go round, in the dark of the moon
my spirit darkens and goes out, and soft strange gloom
pervades my movements and my thoughts and words
then I shall know that I am walking still
with God, we are close together now the moon's in shadow.

*D.H. Lawrence*

108

# Peace

## *A Farm Picture*

Through the ample open door of the peaceful
    country barn,
A sunlit pasture field with cattle and horses feeding,
And haze and vista, and the far horizon fading away.

*Walt Whitman*

# From *The Wish*

Well then! I now do plainly see
This busy world and I shall ne'er agree.
This very honey of all earthly joy
Does of all meats the soonest cloy;
And they, methinks, deserve my pity
Who for it can endure the stings,
The crowd, and buzz, and murmurings,
Of this great hive, the city.

Ah, yet, ere I descend to the grave,
May I a small house and large garden have;
And a few friends, and many books, both true,
Both wise, and both delightful too!
And since love ne'er will from me flee,
A mistress moderately fair,
And good as guardian angels are,
Only beloved and loving me.

How happy here should I
And one dear She live, and embracing die!
She who is all the world, and can exclude,
In deserts, solitude.
I should have then this only fear:
Lest men, when they my pleasures see,
Should hither throng to live like me,
And so make a city here.

*Abraham Cowley*


## *I Share Creation*

When the sun rises, I go to work,
When the sun goes down, I take my rest,
I dig the well from which I drink,
I farm the soil that yields my food,
I share creation, kings can do no more.

*Anonymous Chinese poem*

## From *Lines Written Above Tintern Abbey*

Though absent long,
These forms of beauty have not been to me
As is a landscape to a blind man's eye;
But oft, in lonely rooms, and 'mid the din
Of towns and cities, I have owed to them,
In hours of weariness, sensations sweet,
Felt in the blood, and felt along the heart,
And passing even into my purer mind
With tranquil restoration: feelings too
Of unremembered pleasure: such, perhaps,
As may have had no trivial influence
On that best portion of a good man's life,
His little, nameless, unremembered acts
Of kindness and of love. Nor less, I trust,
To them I may have owed another gift,
Of aspect more sublime: that blessed mood
In which the burthen of the mystery,
In which the heavy and the weary weight
Of all this unintelligible world
Is lightened; that serene and blessed mood
In which the affections gently lead us on

Until, the breath of this corporeal frame
And even the motion of our human blood
Almost suspended, we are laid asleep
In body, and become a living soul;
While with an eye made quiet by the power
Of harmony, and the deep power of joy,
We see into the life of things.

*William Wordsworth*

## Slumber

A slumber did my spirit steal;
I had no human fears:
She seemed a thing that could not feel
The touch of earthly years.

No motion has she now, no force;
She neither hears nor sees;
Rolled round in earth's diurnal course,
With rocks, and stones, and trees.

*William Wordsworth*

## Heaven-Haven: A nun takes the veil

I have desired to go
Where springs not fail,
To fields where flies no sharp and sided hail
And a few lilies blow.

And I have asked to be
Where no storms come,
Where the green swell is in the havens dumb,
And out of the swing of the sea.

*Gerard Manley Hopkins*

# From *Last Hours*

The cool of an oak's unchequered shade
Falls on me as I lie in deep grass
Which rushes upward, blade beyond blade.
While higher the darting grass-flowers pass
Piercing the blue with their crocketed spires
And waving flags, and the ragged fires
Of the sorrel's cresset – a green, brave town
Vegetable, new in renown.

Over the tree's edge, as over a mountain
Surges the white of the moon,
A cloud comes up like the surge of a fountain,
Pressing round and low at first, but soon
Heaving and piling a round white dome.
How lovely it is to be at home
Like an insect in the grass
Letting life pass!

*D.H. Lawrence*

## From *Sabbath Bells*

I've often on a Sabbath day
Where pastoral quiet dwells
Lay down among the new mown hay
To listen distant bells
That beautifully flung the sound
Upon the quiet wind
While beans in blossom breathed around
A fragrance o'er the mind

A fragrance and a joy beside
That never wears away
The very air seems deified
Upon a Sabbath day
So beautiful the flitting wrack
Slow pausing from the eye
Earth's music seemed to call them back
Calm settled in the sky

The ear it lost and caught the sound
Swelled beautifully on
And fitful melody around
Of sweetness heard and gone
I felt such thoughts I yearned to sing
The humming air's delight
That seemed to move the swallow's wing
Into a wilder flight

The butterfly in wings of brown
Would find me where I lay
Fluttering and bobbing up and down
And settling on the hay
The waving blossoms seemed to throw
Their fragrance to the sound
While up and down and loud and low
The bells were ringing round

*John Clare*

## The Tree of Life

The tree of life my soul hath seen,
Laden with fruit and always green:
The trees of nature fruitless be
Compared with Christ the apple tree.

His beauty doth all things excel:
By faith I know, but ne'er can tell
The glory which I now can see
In Jesus Christ the apple tree.

For happiness I long have sought,
And pleasure dearly I have bought:
I missed of all; but now I see
'Tis found in Christ the apple tree.

I'm weary with my former toil,
Here I will sit and rest awhile:
Under the shadow I will be,
Of Jesus Christ the apple tree.

This fruit doth make my soul to thrive,
It keeps my dying faith alive;
Which makes my soul in haste to be
With Jesus Christ the apple tree.

*Compiled by Joshua Smith*

## Comforts from Above

Long may'st thou joy in this almighty love,
Long may thy soul be pleasing in his sight,
Long may'st thou have true comforts from above,
Long may'st thou set on him thy whole delight,
And patiently endure when he doth prove,
Knowing that he will surely do thee right:
Thy patience, faith long-suffering, and thy love,
He will reward with comforts from above.

*Aemilia Lanyer*

## Still Small Voice of Calm

Dear Lord and Father of mankind,
Forgive our foolish ways!
Reclothe us in our rightful mind,
In purer lives thy service find,
In deeper reverence praise.

In simple trust like theirs who heard,
Beside the Syrian sea,
The gracious calling of the Lord,
Let us, like them, without a word
Rise up and follow thee.

O Sabbath rest by Galilee!
O calm of hills above,
Where Jesus knelt to share with thee
The silence of eternity,
Interpreted by love!

Drop thy still dews of quietness,
Till all our strivings cease;
Take from our souls the strain and stress,
And let our ordered lives confess
The beauty of thy peace.

Breathe through the heats of our desire
Thy coolness and thy balm;
Let sense be dumb, let flesh retire;
Speak through the earthquake, wind and fire,
O still small voice of calm!

*John Greenleaf Whittier*

**Sunday**

## Peace

My soul, there is a country
Far beyond the stars,
Where stands a winged sentry
All skilful in the wars:
There above noise and danger
Sweet Peace sits crowned with smiles,
And one born in a manger
Commands the beauteous files.
He is thy gracious friend
And – O my soul, awake! –
Did in pure love descend
To die here for thy sake.
If thou canst get but thither,
There grows the flower of Peace,
The Rose that cannot wither,
Thy fortress, and thy ease.
Leave then thy foolish ranges
For none can thee secure,
But one who never changes,
Thy God, thy life, thy cure.

*Henry Vaughan*

## Psalm 23

God, my shepherd! I don't need a thing.
You have bedded me down in lush meadows,
you find me quiet pools to drink from.
True to your word, you let me catch my breath,
and send me in the right direction.

Even when the way goes through Death Valley,
I'm not afraid when you walk at my side.
Your trusty shepherd's crook makes me feel secure.

You serve me a six-course dinner
right in front of my enemies.
You revive my drooping head;
my cup brims with blessing.

Your beauty and love chase after me
every day of my life.
I'm back home in the house of God
for the rest of my life.

*The Bible*

# First line index

**A**

A slumber did my spirit steal   113
A soft Sea washed around the House   61
Ah, what shall I be at fifty   57
All night long on my bed   79
Amid the smoke of cities did you pass   87
And did you get   77
And if tonight my soul may find   107
Angels, in the early morning   9
As a father has compassion   51

**B**

Be not afraid, O land   27
But now, this is what the Lord says   92

**C**

Consider   30

**D**

Dear Lord and Father of mankind   120
Death, be not proud   105
Does the road wind up-hill all the way   80

**E**

Earth has not anything   11

**F**

Father, father, where are you going   35
For everything there is a season   53
For the beauty of the earth   66
For whatsoever from one place doth fall   43

**G**

Glory be to God for dappled things   62
Go and open the door   40
God moves in a mysterious way   38
God, my shepherd   123
God of the morning   15

**H**

He who bends to himself a joy   59
Here, quiet on this stony shore   106
'Hope' is a thing with feathers   29
How happy is he born and taught   68

## I

I have desired to go   114
I have seen the sun break through   52
I remember before you were born   90
I remember that room so clearly   44
I saw Eternity the other night   45
I shall know why   31
I wonder as I wander   28
I wonder if the sap is stirring yet   26
If ever two were one   85
If I say, 'Surely the darkness will hide me   103
I'll make up for the years of the locust   41
It is good to praise the Lord   70
It is the first mild day of March   23
It was a perfect day   96
It was I who taught Ephraim to walk   89
It's all I have to bring today   14
I've often on a Sabbath day   116

## L

Laid in my quiet bed   54
Long may'st thou joy   119
Love bade me welcome   81

## M

'Man's life is like a Sparrow   47
Most glorious Lord of life   82
My God, my God   101
My heart is like a singing bird   73
My soul, sit thou a patient looker-on   57
My soul, there is a country   122

## N

Now that I've nearly done my days   20
Now you will feel no rain   84

## O

O sweeter than the marriage feast   83
Oh, you gotta get a glory   19
One without looks in tonight   99
Over the land   25

## P

Piping down the valleys wild   60
Praise the Lord from the earth   75
Prayer the Church's banquet   71

## S

Silent is the house   101
Sky and grass – the same colour   98
So early it's still almost dark out   18
Softly, in the dusk   46
Sunset and evening star   104

## T

The chime of the bells   100
The cool of an oak's unchequered shade   115
The curfew tolls the knell of parting day   97
The grey sea and the long black land   78
The heavens declare   13
The little boy lost in the lonely fen   35
The love of God, unutterable and perfect   93
The morns are meeker than they were   22
The poetry of earth is never dead   32
The ring so worn, as you behold   86
The seas are quiet   56
The storm has passed   64
The tree of life my soul hath seen   118
There are nights that are so still   33
Therefore let the moon   95
They might not need me   86
This is the spot   63
Though absent long   112
Through the ample open door   109
Today, I think   74

## W

We grow accustomed to the Dark   102
Well then! I now do plainly see   110
What soul was his   12
What wondrous life is this I lead   65
When I consider how my light is spent   34
When I woke   10
When men were all asleep   16
When the green woods laugh   72
When the sun rises   111
When the white feet of the baby   88
When to the sessions   50
When will the bell ring   55
Where we made the fire   48
Would I might lie like this   36

# Author index

William Blake (1757–1827)   35, 59, 60, 72
Anne Bradstreet (1612–72)   85
Robert Bridges (1844–1930)   16
Emily Brontë (1818–48)   101
Robert Browning (1812–89)   78
Raymond Carver (1939–88)   18, 77
John Clare (1793–1864)   116
Samuel Taylor Coleridge (1772–1834)   83
Abraham Cowley (1618–67)   110
William Cowper (1731–1800)   38
George Crabbe (1754–1832)   86
Dante Alighieri (1265–1321)   93
Emily Dickinson (1806–86)   9, 14, 22, 29,
    31, 61, 86, 102
John Donne (1572–1631)   105
James Elroy Flecker (1884–1915)   36
Thomas Gray (1716–71)   97
Thomas Hardy (1840–1928)   48, 99
George Herbert (1593–1633)   71, 81
Gerard Manley Hopkins (1844–89)   62, 114
Miroslav Holub (1923–98)   40
Henry Howard (1517?–47)   54
John Keats (1795–1821)   32
Aemilia Lanyer (1569–1645)   119
D.H. Lawrence (1885–1930)   10, 46, 55,
    88, 100, 107, 115
Andrew Marvell (1621–78)   65
John Milton (1608–74)   34
Edith Nesbit (1858–1924)   20
F.S. Pierpoint (1835–1917)   66
Francis Quarles (1592–1644)   57
Christina Rossetti (1830–94)   26, 30, 73, 80

William Shakespeare (1564–1616)   50
Andrea Skevington (b. 1963)   44, 64, 90,
    98, 106
Edmund Spenser (1552?–99)   43, 82
Alfred, Lord Tennyson (1809–92)   57, 104
Edward Thomas (1878–1917)   25, 74, 96
R.S. Thomas (1913–2000)   33, 52
Henry Vaughan (1621–95)   45, 122
Edmund Waller (1606–87)   56
Isaac Watts (1674–1748)   15
Walt Whitman (1819–92)   109
John Greenleaf Whittier (1807–92)   120
Sir Henry Wotton (1568–1639)   68
William Wordsworth (1770–1850)   11, 12,
    23, 47, 63, 87, 95, 112, 113

# Acknowledgments

Every effort has been made to trace and contact copyright owners for material used in this book. We apologize for any inadvertent omissions or errors, and would ask those concerned to contact us so that full acknowledgment can be made in the future.

Pages 13, 27, 51, 70, 75, 79, 89, 92, 101, 103: Scripture quotations taken from the *Holy Bible, New International Version*, copyright © 1973, 1978, 1984 International Bible Society. Used by permission of Zondervan and Hodder & Stoughton Limited. All rights reserved. The 'NIV' and 'New International Version' trademarks are registered in the United States Patent and Trademark Office by International Bible Society. Use of either trademark requires the permission of International Bible Society. UK trademark number 1448790.

Pages 18, 77: 'Happiness' and 'Late Fragment' from *All of Us* by Raymond Carver, published by Harvill Press, © Tess Gallagher, 1996. Used by permission of The Random House Group Limited.

Pages 33, 52: 'The Other' and 'The Bright Field' from *Collected Poems* by R.S. Thomas, published by J.M. Dent.

Page 40: 'The Door' by Miroslav Holub, translated from the Czech by Ian Miller, from *Poems Before and After: Collected English Translations*, Bloodaxe Books 1990.

Pages 41, 123: Scripture taken from *The Message*. Copyright © 1993, 1994, 1995, 1996, 2000, 2001, 2002. Used by permission of NavPress Publishing Group.

Page 53: Scripture quotation is from the Revised Standard Version published by HarperCollins Publishers, copyright © 1989 by the Division of Christian Education of the National Council of the Churches of Christ in the USA, and are used by permission. All rights reserved.